For the refreshing presence -K.

Broken
Just for You

Kathy J. McDow

SkrAiber
PUBLISHING SERVICES

Chandler, Arizona

All scripture quotations, unless otherwise indicated, are taken from the King James Version (KJV). Public Domain.

BROKEN JUST FOR YOU

Library of Congress Cataloging-In-Publication Data

McDow, Kathy J.
Broken just for you / Kathy J. McDow.
p. cm

Library of Congress Control Number: 2007925209

10 DIGIT ISBN 0-9772099-3-8
13 DIGIT ISBN 978-0-9772099-3-4

1. Prayers   4. Poetry
2. Communicating with God   5. Prose
3. Inspiration

Cover Design by Bosgraphdesign

Printed in the United Status of the America

SkrAiber
PUBLISHING SERVICES

Chandler, Arizona 85249
www.skraiberpublishing.com

2007925209

Dedication

With this writing I honor my family elders including Mother, Mrs. Jewell C. McDow, whom I thank for giving her best to her husband and children; Uncle, Mr. Elvin L. Ricks, who instilled in me a thirst for learning and envisioning a life beyond; Aunt, Mrs. Frankie B. Simmons, whose soft spoken nature is a wonderful example to emulate; and Uncle, Mr. Willie A. McDow, whose strength and resolve has given way to endurance.

I further dedicate this book to all my siblings including Bev, who has been a subtle strength of passion and caring; George, who has persevered against much adversity; Doug, who so often shares his ministry of humor through a merry heart; Gayle, who is loved by many and sensitive to the concerns of others; Thomas, who continues to minister to fallen angels and their families; Mary, who has so lovingly shared in blessing me with the heart of a mother; and Terrence, whom God has blessed with an attractive spirit for His glory and honor.

Acknowledgements

All Saints of God
for your prayers of intercession

Bishop Alexis A. Thomas
and the Pilgrim Rest Baptist Church Family
for spiritual connection, continued love and support

Dr. Terry and Pastor Judith Crist
and CitiChurch International
for ushering me into a season of refreshing

Dr. Stephen and Pat Rexroat
for being inspirational teachers of faith and formation

Elder Deborah Barber
for being a Godly example, encouragement and love

Elder John Haddix
for being a teacher, mentor, brother and friend

Fuller Southwest and Cohort 2008
for being a loving community of faith and not letting go

Minister Carolyn Watson
for a praying spirit and sharing her passion for Christ

My Publisher, Dr. Patricia Neff
for being my midwife in birthing this project

Reverend William H. Charles, Sr., Pastor Emeritus
for leading, teaching and stirring up gifts while I was yet a child

Pastor Wesley and First Lady Gwendolyn Relf
and Rehoboth Saints Center Church of God in Christ
for spiritual covering, love and support

St. Olaf College - Northfield, Minnesota
for seeds planted many years ago

The Society of St. Vincent de Paul
Phoenix Diocesan Council
for the blessing of service to humanity

Preface

B *roken Just for You* is a response to one of God's many invitations for me to come away with Him. I shall never forget the day that God impressed upon my spirit that I should partake of Holy Communion during my prayer time with Him. I had participated in both receiving and administering the sacrament corporately but never had I done this alone in the presence of my Heavenly Father. What sort of invitation might this be for me to receive Communion in God's presence? What was God calling me to do and how would this simple, yet very powerful act, change my life forever?

Previously, I had erected an altar where I would study the Word, pray, sit still in God's awesome presence and allow Holy Spirit to minister to me. So in obedience to Him here I sat, on this particular day, at my altar while Holy Spirit brought to my mind several passages of Scripture including, "And when he had given thanks, he brake it, and said, Take, eat: this is my body, which is broken for you: this do in remembrance of me (1 Cor. 11:24). Another Scripture followed, "But he was wounded for our transgression." (Isaiah 53:5a). And then another; all referencing the ultimate sacrifice of my Lord and Savior, Jesus Christ.

I was then led to pray concerning how grateful I was that He was wounded just for me. I told the Lord that I was a sinner and He loved me so much that He would endure the pain and suffering of the cross just for me. I thanked God for His love and faithfulness toward me. I thanked Him for mercy and unmerited favor. In this very moment I felt like I was standing in the gap for all of humanity. I was sorrowful and wanted God to know that we were all sorry for what we had done to Him.

And then the moment came when I would take the bread symbolizing Jesus' broken body and I ate it. With this I felt an enormous debt of gratitude that I did not have to physically suffer; however, I was extremely saddened by the fact that Jesus had to suffer. I drank of the cup and had a vision of the blood streaming down Christ's broken body. I began to weep bitterly at the thought of this precious soul giving Himself for me. The tears just kept billowing out as I cried aloud, asking God's forgiveness. I experienced emotion filled with pain and deep contrition coupled with an exuberant joy in celebrating how great is the Father's love for me.

I shall never forget my first Communion with my Heavenly Father. For He allowed me at a moment in time to share in the fellowship of Christ's suffering - not being distracted by others or ministry work. Spiritually I moved to a much deeper place in my relationship with God and I began engaging in this symbolic ritual on a regular basis. Just me and my Father eating together and sharing in His wonderful Gift of love that was broken just for me and for you. I pray this devotional work will minister to all who would receive, as these very words inspired by God, have also ministered unto to me.

Introduction

A Psalm of David declares, "I waited patiently for the LORD; and He inclined to me, and heard my cry (40:1 KJV). As it was with David, God so desires to dwell with us, to fill us with the Light of His glory that we may be able to bear witness to the wonder and awesomeness of His love and power.

A life apart from God is being separated from our energy source. Yet, we find time for everything but being quiet and still before our God. God is always moving, always speaking and always inviting us to sit at His feet and be blessed. But we don't have time due to rigid schedules, our careers, the children, our spouses and all manner of earthly pleasures. And in a world that is as noisy as ours, who can hear from God?

We must be intentional about our time with God. He will speak words of wisdom to bring clarity to complexity; He will speak peace and calm our storms that we might not have fear in any situation; and He will give us each day our daily bread - that portion which is needful so that we are not overwhelmed by the stuff of life. Such grace, hope and love abound in God's presence. If we start today and commit or recommit to a deeper relationship in Christ, we can enjoy a transformation unparalleled by anything we have known. The pages of *Broken Just for You,* with Scriptures from the Holy Bible and inspired devotional writings, will serve as an enticement to being spiritually renewed in the presence of our Lord.

And when he had given thanks, he brake it, and said, Take, eat: this is my body, which is broken for you: this do in remembrance of me.
I Corinthians 11:24

Prepare ye a daily supper
with the Lord Jesus
As often as you do, do this
in remembrance of Him
There is nothing so intimate as
the breaking of bread together
God wants communion with
His children everyday
By example of Jesus Christ,
present yourself broken before God
God, the Potter will mold you and
make you after His will
Pray unto the Father at communion
and wait patiently by His gates
Worship and praise God, the Father
and He shall direct your path
Be strong in the Lord and the strength
of His might
You will need His strength to impart
to His people
Some will receive the impartation and
some will labor long
God has chosen you to labor
together with them
Blessed be the sweet communion of God
the Father, Son and Holy Spirit

Now therefore fear the LORD, and serve him in sincerity and in truth: and put away the gods which your fathers served on the other side of the flood, and in Egypt; and serve ye the LORD.
Joshua 24:14

Think only of me for thou
shall have no other Gods
Come to me when I call you
and do not tarry
You must do as I say when I
say, "Do this!"
This will please your Father
and you will be blessed
Go fasting and praying also
in the Spirit
Honor your Father with much
sacrifice that He may come
unto you
Watch, fasting and praying and see
the handiwork of your God
The power of the Lord is in your
praise!

Behold, I will do a new thing; now it shall spring forth; shall ye not know it? I will even make a way in the wilderness, and rivers in the desert.
Isaiah 43:19

Hear now the voice
        of the Lord
Incline thine ear only to me
I am come for you, prepare
        now to do a new thing
Whatsoever ye doeth, I will
        be with you until the end
Praise ye God, Jehovah until
        the Spirit of the Lord is
        strong and mighty
Stretch out your hands to touch
        those in need
Feel my Spirit living big in you
        to do great and mighty things
You have my healing power
        the Lord, your God has given
        you healing power
Glorify your God with these
        things and magnify His name

Take my yoke upon you, and learn of me; for I am meek and lowly in heart: and ye shall find rest unto your souls.
Matthew 11:29

Give yourself to me that I may
do these works
The works of your Father are
strong and mighty
Give yourself to me wholly
and completely
That I may live in you to do
good works
Be faithful unto me all the
days of your life
I will be your God and
rescue you
You will come and
go with me
You will reign with
me forever
You are my loveliness, a
bright and morning star
I want you to shine your light
before the people
The Lord is pleased when
you walk in His light

For the LORD will not forsake his people for his great name's sake: because it hath pleased the LORD to make you his people.
I Samuel 12:22

I have not left you, I am performing
a great work in you

Continue to mature in the knowledge
of your God

Be careful for nothing but in all things
through prayer and supplication
make your requests known

I will hear you as you have obeyed me
and you have glorified me

You have made witness of me and
I am pleased

Serve your God with gladness in all
things for you have prospered much

B oth riches and honour come of thee, and thou reignest over all; and in thine hand is power and might; and in thine hand it is to make great, and to give strength unto all.
I Chronicles 29:12

Now I will bring forth
    riches untold
You must share these to do
    the work of your Father
You have been obedient
    to my word
I will not hide my face
    from you
You will have much peace
    in the Lord
You will know much happiness
    in the Son
Sing unto Him who has
    given you life
Sing unto Him new songs
    of praise
Serve the Lord with gladness,
    giving thanks
Have mercy on those who
    cannot hear me
You must love them as I
    have loved you
Then they will see me,
    know me and hear my voice
I will come to you to do this thing

Call unto me, and I will answer thee, and show thee great and mighty things, which thou knowest not.
Jeremiah 33:3

D o you think that I would place you
in a situation you could not bear?
Call out to me and I will show you things
which you know not of
Seek me first in all things and be not
confounded for I bring wisdom
Pray always for the people of God's eyes
to be opened and understanding of my
words
As they turn to me, leaning not to their own
understanding, they shall see miracles
The hand of God is upon them who love
Him and diligently seek him
Walk in the Light of this world and thirst after
His lovingkindness, goodness and mercy
Unto Him be all glory, power and praise
He will bring you perfect peace
Look to Jesus and be encouraged for great is
His faithfulness

But as many as received Him, to them gave He power to become the sons of God, even to them that believe on His Name:
John 1:2

Receive now my cleansing power
I have given this power that you may
become my daughter

I am Almighty God, your Heavenly Father
I give to you the gift of salvation
I give to you a measure of faith
I give to you my Holy Spirit

It is by these you will be victorious
in all things
Boast not, as these are gifts from your
Father because He loves you

Tell the people about my gifts
Share your gifts with the people
in the name of Jesus

This will please me and I shall call
you my child

⮵⮴

How then shall they call on him in whom they have not believed? and   how shall they believe in him of whom they have not heard? and how shall they hear without a preacher?
Romans 10:14

⮵⮴

You will speak my word
    to the masses
You will speak my words
    to those that are near
But you must wait to hear
    my word
You must wait in total
    submission
I will make plain the word
    from on high
You will be my messenger,
    a messenger of God
You will be my witness of
    great might and strength
    in your God
I have chosen you, kept you
    and healed you for this time
This is my appointed time to
    tell of a risen Savior and show
    forth His love
Listen in the stillness and quietness
    for your Lord
I will come for you and you will
    show forth your Father in
    the earth
They shall behold my glory

Which things also we speak, not in the words which man's wisdom teacheth, but which the Holy Ghost teacheth; comparing spiritual things with spiritual.
I Corinthians 2:13

I am the only wise teacher
Come unto me and I will give you
  the knowledge of your Father
Be it unto you to seek ye first the
  Kingdom of God and His righteousness
  and all will be added unto you
In everything give thanks, for this is the
  will of your Father

Trust in me alone, lean not to your
  own understanding
You are fighting a good fight
  Continue in your walk in the Spirit
Continue to glorify me and tell of the
  good news of the Son, Jesus Christ
Sing praises unto the Lord for He is good
  and I will hear thee

G o ye therefore, and teach all nations, baptizing them in the name of the Father, and of the Son, and of the Holy Ghost: (20)Teaching them to observe all things whatsoever I have commanded you: and, lo, I am with you always, even unto the end of the world. Amen.
Matthew 28:19-20

You will continue to grow in
  the knowledge of your God
Walking after His righteousness and
  speaking forth His truth

Be not deceived, God is not mocked
    for in due season you shall reap
    a harvest of blessings
Be obedient to that which I have
    commanded of you and fear only me

I will reward you accordingly, for great
    is mine meat and provision
Go into all the world, preach the Gospel
    and baptize in the name of the Father,
    Son and Holy Spirit

Lo, I am with you always, even
    until the end
Glorify the name of your Father in heaven
    for He brings every good and perfect gift
Be lead of His Spirit in all things and forget
    not His benefits

But ye shall receive power, after that the HolyGhost is come upon you: and ye shall be witnesses unto me both in Jerusalem, and in all Judaea, and in Samaria, and unto the uttermost part of the earth.

Acts 1:8

There is power in the blood and
    name of Jesus
Be not afraid of this thing I have
    given unto you
For it is far greater than anything
    known to you
It is far greater than the power of
    any man
The evil one cannot stand against
    this power
It is my Spirit I have poured out
    upon you

You shall have Holy Ghost power
    to walk not in this world but
    in the marvelous Light
People will know me as I speak
    through you
They will know me as I touch
    through you
The will know me as I heal
    through you
You will bring glory to my name
    in your obedience
Hear my voice, go and do as I have
    commanded you to do

O Lord GOD, thou hast begun to shew thy
servant thy greatness, and thy mighty hand: for
what God is there in heaven or in earth, that can do
according to thy works, and according to thy might?

Deuteronomy 3:24

G od will use you mightily,
    wait by His gates
Listen for the voice
    of your God
Who knoweth all things,
    seeth and worketh all things

It is He who hath fashioned us
    and not we ourselves
Greater is He that is in us than
    he that is in the world
We shall honor our Lord and
    God of the ages

We shall sing praises to the
    King of Kings
He shall protect and hide us
    from danger
He will be our banner, our shield
    and our fortress

Some will not hear our testimony
    and come against us
We will prevail for Almighty God
    is on our side

And I saw a new heaven and a new earth: for the first heaven and the first earth were passed away; and there was no more sea. (2) And I John saw the holy city, new Jerusalem, coming down from God out of heaven, prepared as a bride adorned for her husband.
Revelation 21:1-2

I have called forth a mighty woman of God
a woman after my own heart
A woman with eyes to see and ears to hear
what thus saith her God

She is mine and mine alone, she is my bride
and mother of all nations
She will pray my kingdom come on earth
I will hear and answer if she seeks my face

I will heal her soul's diseases and prosper her
lands until that day
A day when every knee shall bow and tongue
confess that Jesus is Lord

A day when all men will stand before an
Almighty God with fear and trembling
She will prepare them to be ready
when I shall come

K now therefore this day, and consider it in thine heart, that the LORD he is God in heaven above, and upon the earth beneath: there is none else.
Deuteronomy 4:39

I am the Lord, God Almighty
        there is none like me
All power in Heaven and earth
        is mine
I will pour out my anointing on
        the children of God
If you will hear my voice, you
        will do as I command

Ask anything, believing you have
        received and you shall
My children shall not suffer lack
        your Father has more than enough
Take it, use it to bring glory
        to my name
Show to others what I have
        given unto you

Praise ye the Lord for He is good
Praise ye the Lord for He suffers long
Praise ye the Lord for He careth for you

Come now and let us reason together

T hen Jesus answering said unto them, Go your way, and tell John what things ye have seen and heard; how that the blind see, the lame walk, the lepers are cleansed, the deaf hear, the dead are raised, to the poor the gospel is preached.
Luke 7:22

I bring healing and peace
　　to a dying world
The problem is, they cannot
　　see or hear me
This is where my children
　　come in
My children must tell those
　　who are blind to me
My children must tell those
　　who are deaf to me

My children must tell these
　　that I love them
My children must tell these
　　of my abundance
There is room in mine house
　　for all of these
Children of God, go and bring
　　them unto me

I will reward my children, according
　　each one, to his measure of works
Great is the reward of your Father
　　in heaven
Unto God be all glory, honor and
　　praise
Tell them it is so ....

❦

L et not your heart be troubled: ye believe in God,
believe also in me. (2)In my Father's house are
many mansions: if it were not so, I would have told
you. I go to prepare a place for you.
John 14:1-2

❦

L et not your heart
be troubled
Ye believe in God,
believe also in me
In my Father's house are
many mansions
If it were not so, I would
have told you
I go to prepare a place for you
and if I go, I will come again
and receive you unto me
That where I am,
there ye may be also

Repent, for the Kingdom of God
is at hand
He shall come with mighty force
and like a thief
Be ye ready when the Son of
man shall come
He will come to gather all that
belong to Him
To be with Him, His children in
glory, forever

Let us come before his presence with thanksgiving, and make a joyful noise unto him with psalms.
Psalms 95:2

L et the Church of God
      say Amen
Let them hear the voice
    of their God
Let them come before Him
    with fear and trembling
Let them honor Him with
    praise and thanksgiving
The Lord, your God is great
    and greatly to be praised

Obey the voice of your God and
    become one with His Spirit
That you may dwell in the unity
    of your faith
Mighty is your power in unity
    seek the Lord of all for your wisdom
Be still, wait upon God and move
    in the Spirit of unity
He will not forsake His people,
    who by their witness
will have much success

In God we shall come into the knowledge
    and prosper in unity
Be it unto the Church to give Him glory!

T he LORD is gracious, and full of compassion;
slow to anger, and of great mercy.
Psalms 145:8

S peak only the words of
    your Father
Your words must show forth
    the goodness of your God
Evil hath no place in the mind
    of God's children
Speak of love and tender mercies
    all the day long

Be slow to judge and swift to
    love
Give unto others as God has
    given unto you
A humbled heart is the pleasure
    of your Father
He doeth all things well even in
    the face of adversity

You cannot always know His
    ways
Believe Him for the victories in
    Christ Jesus
For all work together for good to
    them that love Him
Let not the evil one cause you to
    stumble by your tongue

Speak only of the goodness of God
all the day long!

And God said unto Moses, I AM THAT I AM:
and he said, Thus shalt thou say unto the
children of Israel, I AM hath sent me unto you.
Exodus 3:14

I am sharpening your focus so that you
concentrate only on me
Whatever you need, desire or you're
concerned about - *I AM THAT!*

If you want more love -
I AM THE CHRIST
If you want more joy -
I AM YOUR DELIGHT
If you want more peace -
I AM YOUR STILL WATER
If you want more wisdom -
I AM MY HOLY WORD
If you're in need of healing -
I AM THE GREAT PHYSICIAN
If you're in need of restoration -
I AM A BULWARK NEVER FAILING
If you're in need of direction
I AM A LAMP UNTO YOUR FEET

Look to the hills from whence cometh
your help
All your help comes from me, your Lord
God Almighty
Rejoice and be glad for - *I AM!*

Then Moses said unto Aaron, This is it that the LORD spake, saying, I will be sanctified in them that come nigh me, and before all the people I will be glorified. And Aaron held his peace.
Leviticus 10:3

Be silent before your Father,
  bow down and worship Him
He is greatly to be praised,
  bless His holy name in the temple
You have been sanctified to do the
  will of your Father
Rejoice, for mighty is the hand
  of your God
He liveth in you to worketh all
  things well
Be of good cheer and magnify
  His name always
Great is the reward to them that
  know Him and obey His voice
You shall reap a harvest in due season
  Wait, walk and faint not for He is nigh
He will come like a rushing mighty wind
  and receive you unto Him

Whosoever believeth that Jesus is the Christ is born of God: and every one that loveth him that begat loveth him also that is begotten of him
I John 5:1

Go tell it on the mountain,
   tell it everywhere
Go tell it on the mountain,
   that Jesus Christ is born
This is my message to the world

Deliver this message to all who will hear
   for they shall be called my children
And they shall receive my Holy
   Ghost power
This power, the world cannot give
   For it is my power, mighty and strong
Power to do all things in the name of the
   Father, Son and Holy Spirit

Go tell it on the mountain,
   even if they don't receive
Your Father delights in your witness
   and in them that receive
Rejoice together with the Spirit of
   the Living God in unity

F or God so loved the world, that he gave his only begotten Son, that whosoever believeth in him should not perish, but have everlasting life.
John 3:16

Be thou my love forever
    and ever
One who was created by
    my hands in my image
See me with your eyes and
    hear with your ears
The greatest gift I give unto
    my lovely child
Treasure this gift that sets
    you apart
But nevertheless a gift that
    can be had by all who will
    call upon my name
Others too, may receive my
    treasure and be set apart
That you may all reign together
    with the Son
Now that you have received,
    be fruitful and extend yourself
    to others
There is room for many in your
    Father's house
Give them my gift and they shall
    come to me

I will praise thee, O LORD, with my whole heart; I
will shew forth all thy marvellous works. (2)I will
be glad and rejoice in thee: I will sing praise to thy
name, O thou most High.
Psalms 9:1-2

Y ou must bring glory
    to your Father
You must bring glory, honor
    and praise to your Father
I will give to you my words from
    on High - speak them!
I will give to you songs from
    on High - sing them!
I will give to you power from
    on High - use it!

Bring glory, honor and praise
    to Almighty God
Forget not the hand that
    made you
Forget not the hand that
    delivered you
Forget not the lovingkindness
    and mercies of your Father
Be ready when I call upon you to
    show forth my glory in the earth

Be humble and holy in the power
    and might of your God
Praise ye the Lord!

Praise ye the LORD. Praise God in his sanctuary: praise him in the firmament of his power.
Psalms 150:1

There is no greater love than the
    love I have for my children
I have everything they need and
    want to give all to them
Tell them to seek me first in all
    things that all be given unto them
They shall be healed and made whole
    by the power of their praise
Sing of the joy of your salvation by
    the Son, Christ Jesus
Sing of the power and might of God,
    the Father
Sing praises unto the Holy One, the
    only wise One who is your teacher
Enter into the presence of the Lord
    singing praises and worship with
    your whole being
You shall be delivered and made whole
    by your praise

Then there shall be a place which the LORD your
God shall choose to cause his name to dwell
there; thither shall ye bring all that I command you;
your burnt offerings, and your sacrifices, your tithes,
and the heave offering of your hand, and all your
choice vows which ye vow unto the LORD:
Deuteronomy 12:11

Thou shall have no other
    God before me
Lay all your sacrifices
    upon the altar
Sacrifice these things in a
    spirit of obedience
For this will greatly please
    your Father
Your Father knoweth all,
    doeth all and giveth all
You will bring little in your
    sacrifice but will receive much
The Lord desires to satisfy His
    children when they obey
Bring the sacrifice to the altar and
    give it unto God
He shall restore your soul and make
    you to lie down in green pastures
Great is the reward to them that
    giveth all things unto the Father
He is faithful and just and His
    mercy endureth

Casting all your care upon him; for he careth for you.

I Peter 5:7

Your ways are not my ways
    I am here to accomplish all you
      cannot do
I am here to care for you for
    I am your God

You are here to delight in me
You are here to know joy and have
    strength in me
By my Spirit you are to praise and
    worship me

Let my Spirit lead you in the
    things of me
You are here to be set apart and
    to live Holy
I am here to redeem and forgive
    your sins

You are never alone for I live in you
    All that you need lives within you
Great and mighty is your Father,
    who cares for His children

S ubmit yourselves therefore to God. Resist the
devil, and he will flee from you.
James 4:7

I am greater than anything that
    your mind can conceive
Evil will come against you but
    the battle is not yours
Surrender your all to me and I
    will hide you
You will wrestle in your spirit
    with the evil one
Be not afraid, for I have given
    you power

In the name of Jesus, he must flee
In the name of Jesus, he must bow
In the name of Jesus, he cannot harm

Keep your thoughts toward
    your God
Know your power by my word
    and speak it
I will rebuke the devourer for my
    name sake
A mighty fortress is your God,
    run to the tower and I will hide you

The LORD shall establish thee an holy people unto himself, as he hath sworn unto thee, if thou shalt keep the commandments of the LORD thy God, and walk in his ways.

Deuteronomy 28:9

In the quiet stillness
 I will speak to you
In dreams and visions
 I will speak to you
Commit thy ways unto the
 God of your salvation
Commit thy ways unto me

You will set the captives free
 in my name
Because I have loved you, you
 will love them

Tell them of my saving grace
Tell them of my healing power
Tell them of my Holy Ghost power

You must seek my face to do
 this thing
And forget not who is with you
 to do all things
Give God glory, forgetting not
 the might of His hand

For many are called, but few are chosen.
Matthew 22: 14

Chosen are they,
who from *before* their existence,
knew me
Chosen are they,
who from *before* their existence,
walked with me
Chosen are they,
who from *before* their existence,
received *power* of creation
Chosen are they,
who from *before* their existence,
received *knowledge* of my Word
Chosen are they,
who from *before* their existence,
received the *fullness* of their God
Chosen are they,
who from *before* their existence,
were *mighty* in battle against evil
Chosen are they,
who from *before* their existence,
were the *righteous* remnant
Chosen are they,
who from *before* their existence,
delighted to *praise* God at all times
Called are they,
who from *before* their existence,
to be *led* of His chosen into all truth

❧❧❧❧❧❧

But he was wounded for our transgressions, he was bruised for our iniquities: the chastisement of our peace was upon him; and with his stripes we are healed.

Isaiah 53:5

Jesus died for you, it is by His
  blood you are healed
Receive ye now, this blood bought
  gift of healing
I see you and feel your pain

It is by the flesh of His flesh
It is by the bone of His bone
That your Father can feel your pain

Know that your Father loves you
  as He has loved the Son
I am come that you would return
  unto me
You will know my power by my Spirit

Rejoice in the Lord, your God. I will
  bring forth that which was dead
You are resurrected with the Son unto
  life everlasting
All things are possible through this Son

For he is our God; and we are the people of his pasture, and the sheep of his hand. Today if ye will hear his voice, (8) Harden not your heart, as in the provocation, and as in the day of temptation in the wilderness:

Psalms 95: 7-8

My sheep know my voice
They can know me by my Word
They can know me by my Spirit

Happy is the man who delights in his God
Happy is he who obeys his God
Happy is he who will praise his God

Your joy and strength are in the Lord
Your peace and love are in the Lord
Your hope and power are in the Lord

The day of our Lord is upon us
He has come to set us free
Those who know His voice will be free

You can know His peace and joy
Acknowledge the Lord today!
Say completely yes to His will

He will come for all who will receive
Be ye ready when the Lord, Jesus shall come
We will reign together with our Lord

But Jesus said, Suffer little children, and forbid them not, to come unto me: for of such is the kingdom of heaven.

Matthew 19:14

Enter in as little children
for such is the Kingdom
Come before His presence with
fear and trembling
Present your body a living sacrifice
holy and acceptable
Thou shalt have no other gods
before God, Almighty
Thou shalt not worship any other
thing in heaven or earth
Wait upon the Lord, your God
to receive a fresh anointing
After this, the Holy Ghost will
come upon you
Listen and obey the Word of the
Lord as He brings forth
Do not ignore this gift of power
in the Spirit
It is by His power you will overcome
in the earth
It is by His power you will cast
out evil
It is by His power you shall honor
and glorify the Father
As a child seeks his earthly father, so shall
you seek your Heavenly Father

And Jesus said unto them, Because of your unbelief: for verily I say unto you, If ye have faith as a grain of mustard seed, ye shall say unto this mountain, Remove hence to yonder place; and it shall remove; and nothing shall be impossible unto you.

Matthew 17:20

S top doubting the Word of
your Father
I am not a man that I should
lie
I come to bring abundance into
your life
I come to bring every good and
perfect gift into your life
You must believe when you
ask of me
You must believe and you shall
have what you ask

"Little faith can bring much!"

Speak to your mountains
that they be moved
Speak to evil that it must
flee
Do this all in the name of Jesus,
the Son
When you believe in His power
it pleases your Father
Speak now to your mountains
that they be removed
Speak life that you may live
and not die

And he said, Take heed that ye be not deceived: for many shall come in my name, saying, I am Christ; and the time draweth near: go ye not therefore after them.

Luke 21:8

Many will come to you
    now in my name
Ask of your Father
    if it is so
Ask of your Father and
    I will lead you in all truth
Ask of your Father that you
    may have wisdom
Guard your tongue and speak
    not without the hand of God
To them that would come to you,
    shine my light
Delight in me to bring forth
    my glory

Love your brother and your enemy
Pray for your brother and your enemy

Then you shall glorify your Father
    and the Son
Entreat the Holy One as you go, for
    you are never alone
Listen in the stillness of His Spirit
    at all times
You are an overcomer by the Spirit
    of the Living God
You shall know them by their fruit
    and God shall be the judge

For God hath not given us the spirit of fear; but of power, and of love, and of a sound mind.
II Timothy 1:7

True children of God
      are fearless
For they have been given
      a Spirit of power and love
God's children must walk by
      faith and not by sight
God's children must be
      steadfast and unmovable
God's children must choose
      whom they will serve
God's children must be
      forever faithful
God's children hath received
      the Son and His power
God's children will reign together
      with the Son
Go into all the world as sons
      and daughters of the Most High
Preach, baptize, teach all in the
      name of Jesus, the Son
Show forth His might, mercy and
      lovingkindness to those living
      in the dark
JESUS IS THE LIGHT!

And I will bring an everlasting reproach upon you, and a perpetual shame, which shall not be forgotten.

Jeremiah 23:40

Beware of those who come
    in my name
Saying thus saith the Lord,
    God of hosts
You shall know them by
    my Holy Word
Hear their voices and ask of
    me what thus saith

Woe unto them who practice
    deceit in my name
For they shall be cut off
    from prosperity
They shall be cut off from the
    land the Lord giveth
They shall go out and not
    come in
They shall be made ashamed and
    not be forgotten of evil

These are my people who would
    humble themselves
These are mine who would seek
    my face in repentance
I WILL HEAR AND SPEAK
TO THESE........

Trust in the LORD with all thine heart; and lean not unto thine own understanding. In all thy ways acknowledge him, and he shall direct thy paths.

Proverbs 3:5-6

When you go, go only in the name
　　of your Father
When you speak, speak only in the
　　name of your Father
When you pray, pray only in the
　　name of Jesus
When you see, see only by the
　　power of the Spirit

When you walk in the Spirit of His
　　Holiness, you are made right
　　with Him
When you walk in the Spirit of His
　　Holiness, you are made one
　　with Him
Be careful not to show forth your
　　hand as the hand of God
Unto the God of the ages be all
　　power, glory, honor and praise

And blessed is she that believed: for there shall be a performance of those things which were told her from the Lord. (46) And Mary said, My soul doth magnify the Lord, (47) And my spirit hath rejoiced in God my Saviour.
Luke 1: 45-47

Lord, I see the progression of how you drew me to you and loved me to you. Even in my affliction, were you present to lift me up and restore my soul. I am eternally grateful for your lovingkindness and faithfulness toward me.

Ever so gently you have fed me on the milk of your Word and rocked me in the cradle of your Spirit. I am refreshed and renewed. My soul magnifies the Lord for you have delivered me out of bondage. Yes, I have been set free by the blood of Jesus! Hallelujah!

It is now I am being made ready to work for my Master. You are now feeding me with the meat of your Word and giving to me your desires and vision. I praise you for your mighty acts of mercy. Thank you for honoring me and loving me so much. Amen.

For the LORD thy God hath chosen him out of all
thy tribes, to stand to minister in the name of the
LORD, him and his sons for ever.
Deuteronomy 18:5

Thank you, Oh Lord
    for choosing me
at this appointed time
    in this appointed place
    among these appointed people

Thank you, Oh Lord
    that you are ever refining me
    and transforming me
    into the likeness of your Son

I shall wait for the
    voice of my God and
    upon His Spirit
    that I may speak and move

Give to me, Oh God
    all things......
    that I may give these
    unto all people of all nations

*We will sing Glory Hallelujah to our
risen Lord!*

K now therefore that the LORD thy God, he is God, the faithful God, which keepeth covenant and mercy with them that love him and keep his commandments to a thousand generations;
Deuteronomy 7:9

I have not forgotten you
  for I am your God
Though you cannot see me
  I worketh all things
Your love is a love that is
  ever changing
My love is a love that is
  ever unfailing
Come, be my unfailing love
  and walk with me
Worship me all the day long
  in spirit and truth
I, your Father and your God shall
  deliver thee out of darkness
You will be one with my
  marvelous Light
To bear all things, believe all things
  and accomplish all in the name of
    I AM!

By this shall all men know that ye are my disciples, if ye have love one to another.
John 13:35
Grtfr43

I will make plain your path
    as you continue in prayer
  and fasting
Great are those in need
    of my lovingkindness
I have given you this to give
    it also unto these
My heart is a heart after
    all people
You cannot love some who
    are more lovely
You must love all my people
    with my heart
This love will make them
    whole and complete
This love will bring new and
    abundant life
This love will never leave or
    forsake them
This love will never fail them,
    is gentle and longsuffering
This love is pure, true and boldly
    seeks action
Give this love to all my people -
    the love I have given unto you

So then faith cometh by hearing, and hearing by the word of God.

Romans 10:17

J oy cometh to them believing
   they have received
Faith cometh to them believing
   they have heard
By faith we are saved and
   transformed into newness
By faith those things which are not
   are made manifest
God is able to do exceeding and
   abundant above what you ask

Faith pleases your God and Savior
Faith can bring joy in the midst of sorrow
Faith can restore that which was lost
Faith can bring healing to the sick

Rejoice in the Lord and have faith in God
Know that He is good and His mercy endures

Rejoice, Rejoice, Rejoice!

But they that wait upon the LORD shall renew their strength; they shall mount up with wings as eagles; they shall run, and not be weary; and they shall walk, and not faint.

Isaiah 40:31

The Lord is pleased with your
    waiting upon Him
You are not ashamed of the
    Gospel of Jesus Christ
Build up your faith and continue
    to share the Good News
Tell of His goodness and mercy,
    kindness and patience
Tell of His saving grace and
    His desire to bless
Show others His heart, His
    light and His works
Boast not of the things of God
    be careful to give Him all praise
Go not before the Lord, your God
    but go after Him
He will guide you in all truth, bearing
    all things and suffering all things
It is only by Him that all will
    be saved
It is only by Him that all things
    are possible

S ojourn in this land, and I will be with thee, and will bless thee; for unto thee, and unto thy seed, I will give all these countries, and I will perform the oath which I sware unto Abraham thy father;
Genesis 26:3

I am restoring unto you
　your covering
You shall no longer
　　be desolate
The land which the Lord giveth
　　shall be called blessed
The people shall be called the
　　children of God
They must worship only the
　　true and Living God
I have sent them leaders after
　　mine own heart
Go and tell them of the cost
　　of idol worship
For I will turn my face from
　　them everyone
The darkness will overtake them
　　for their hearts will be hard
If they would worship the Lord
　　I will move in their favor
I will bless and increase them
　　I will bless their inheritance

That I may shew forth all thy praise in the gates of the daughter of Zion: I will rejoice in thy salvation. (15)The heathen are sunk down in the pit that they made: in the net which they hid is their own foot taken.
Psalms 9:14-15

Oh, daughter of Zion
    come out from among them
You must be set apart for High
    and Holy is your God
You shall be as precious jewels
    among the ruins
The people will know and see
    the beauty of the Lord
Obey the Word of your God
    and receive power
Power to live righteous and
    holy without fear
Power to proclaim the Gospel
    of Jesus to the heathens
Power to lead God's children
    out of bondage
The Lord has chosen, appointed
    and anointed you
Fear not for I am with you
    always
Great is your Lord in all of
    Heaven and earth
He changeth not and is more
    than enough
Well able to do exceeding and
    abundantly above all

That thine alms may be in secret: and thy Father which seeth in secret himself shall reward thee openly.

Matthew 6:4

Your prayer sacrifices and
    sacrifices of fasting will
    bring you Godly wisdom
For what you will do in secret,
    He will reward you openly
Do not say, "I have brought
    my sacrifices to Almighty
    God for His sake!"
Your father is the great I AM
    and lacks nothing in
    Heaven or earth
Your sacrifices will draw you
    closer to your Father that
    you may receive revelation
The Lord is well pleased
    by your offering and
    your reward will be great
You shall be exalted in the
    Kingdom of God
    in due season
No hurt or harm shall come
    nigh to thee in
    the time of trouble
You shall reign together with
    Jesus forever and ever

And thou shalt teach them ordinances and laws, and shalt shew them the way wherein they must walk, and the work that they must do.
Exodus 18:20

I will lead you in all things of me
You shall be my teacher of the people
You will teach them of your Father's mercy
You will teach them of your Father's grace
You will teach them of your Father's love
You will pray unto your Father
After this, the Holy Ghost shall come upon you

Teach of your God's ways in the Spirit
Lean not to your own understanding
Allow God to direct your path to His gates
Enter to praise and worship Almighty God
Depart to serve all people of every nation
Serve those who are the spiritually dead
Tell these especially, of the love of your Father

How then shall they call on him in whom they have not believed? and how shall they believe in him of whom they have not heard? and how shall they hear without a preacher? (15)And how shall they preach, except they be sent? as it is written, How beautiful are the feet of them that preach the gospel of peace, and bring glad tidings of good things!

Romans 10:14-15

By Divine order I shall send
   you to your covering
He shall know you by
   my Spirit
He shall be your father,
   after Me, in the earth
Be obedient to him that would
   reprove you for my name sake
This will strengthen you in me,
   your Heavenly Father
Be mindful always of my Spirit
   living in you
You will know of his teachings
   by my Spirit
Pray for him that he would
   follow after me
You shall do great things and
   bring honor to my name
I will be pleased and reward
   thee accordingly -
Both the teacher and the man of God

He that believeth on me, as the scripture hath said, out of his belly shall flow rivers of living water.

John 7:38

I fill your cup with living
water, drink ye all of it
It shall be nourishment to your soul

I give to you my Spirit,
    take in all of Him
He shall be meat to thy flesh

I give to you my sight, see all
    through the eyes of Me
It shall testify to the wonders
    of your Father

I give to you my love,
    let me flow through you
By this shall all know you are
    mine, my child

I give to you my power,
    speak forth deliverance
It shall be healing to the sick, sight
for the blind, legs for the lame

I give to you dominion
    over all creation
It shall be your dwelling place for a season

**Then I shall come for you and we will
reign together forever and ever
Hallelujah!**

A nd I have filled him with the spirit of God, in
wisdom, and in understanding, and in
knowledge, and in all manner of workmanship
Exodus 31:3

I am taking you to higher heights
 in Christ Jesus
You are growing in the knowledge
 of your God
Pray unto the Holy One for
 revelation of my Word
It shall be made plain unto you
 by the Spirit of the Lord
You will honor the Father and
 obey His Word
You are my light in the earth
 before men
Go in the earth to let this light
 shine
Be consumed over and within by the
 power of the Spirit
Then men will see the light and
 glorify me
This is my purpose to my beloved
 daughter
You are not alone to do this thing
 I am with you always, until the end
It well pleases your Father to do this
 thing, to shine His light

But sanctify the Lord God in your hearts: and be ready always to give an answer to every man that asketh you a reason of the hope that is in you with meekness and fear

I Peter 3:15

Always be ready with a word
    from the Lord
Those who practice to deceive
    will not be able to stand
In the face of an Almighty God,
    they will not prevail
As the Spirit leadeth, testify of
    His power and majesty
As the Spirit leadeth, give utterance
    of signs and wonders
Resist the evil one and he will
    surely flee
Pray God's blessings upon him that
    would receive
To him that continues in darkness,
    rebuke in the name of Jesus
You shall know my children
    through me
Love these with my heart for these
    are your brothers
The Spirit within you shall cleave
    unto the Spirit within them
You are all one in the Spirit of your
    Lord and Savior
By this shall all know your are mine!

❦❧❦❧❦❧

He that spared not his own Son, but delivered him up for us all, how shall he not with him also freely give us all things?
Romans 8:32

Have I not delivered thee up
    up from the mire?
Am I not a man that I
    should lie?
Be careful for nothing, make
    your requests known
For I am the God who giveth
    all things
I am the God who doeth
    all things
Whatsoever things ye desire
    I will give unto you
Believe in the Lord and the
    power of His might
Sparing not His own Son, how
    shall He not give unto you?
Believe that all things are possible-
    only believe
I am the great I Am and you
    are my child
I love you as I have loved the Son,
    you are joint heirs together
You shall be like Him in that day
    and the glory of the Lord shall
        be unto you

For ye are bought with a price: therefore glorify God in your body, and in your spirit, which are God's.

I Corinthians 6:20

I want all of you, no part shall
    be left unto its own
You are mine, wholly and
    completely you shall be mine
Incline thine ear, give me your
    thoughts, give me your heart
I want your mind, soul and body,
    wholly and completely give
    them to me
Acknowledge the Lord your God
    in all that you do and say
Seek my face concerning all things
    great and small - all things
Wait patiently upon the Lord, your
    God and I will come to show
    you all things
Great and mighty things shall I give
    unto you in Jesus name
I will be lifted high and glorified in
    all heaven and earth
    By the Son living in you!

Even the Spirit of truth; whom the world cannot receive, because it seeth him not, neither knoweth him: but ye know him; for he dwelleth with you, and shall be in you.

John 14:17

You can hear me but cannot
    see me
You can feel me but cannot
    be me
I am all 'round, ever present
    with you
Rejoice in me and I will give
    you peace
Blessed are they that hunger
    and thirst for Jesus
They shall all be filled with
    His Spirit
They shall all know of his
    saving grace
They shall all be called my
    children
I shall freely give unto these
    all things
They shall be set free by
    the power
They shall prosper in Jesus
    by His blood
They shall have my wisdom
    by His Spirit
They shall know the Father
    by His Son

And when he had called the people unto him with his disciples also, he said unto them, Whosoever will come after me, let him deny himself, and take up his cross, and follow me.
Mark 8:34

They that wait upon the Lord
  shall be renewed
Behold the newness of your
  life in Jesus
In the morning when you rise,
  give yourself to Jesus
He will go with you that you
  may not stumble
See the world with His eyes
  that you may understand truth
Love others with His heart that
  they may know Him
Speak only those words He would
  give unto you
Do only those things He would
  ask of you
You will have joy and much
  success in Him
Remember your Creator and
  in all things give thanks
Walk not before Him but after
  the power of His might

But he was wounded for our transgressions, he was bruised for our iniquities: the chastisement of our peace was upon him; and with his stripes we are healed.

Isaiah 53:5

Healing is a gift from your
    Father
Healing in your body and
    healing in your soul
Your Father has what you need
    and you shall lack no good thing
There is healing in the peace
    of your God
There is healing in the knowledge
    of your God
There is healing in the Word
    of your God
Run to Him and receive your gift
    be thankful and bless His name
You have been resurrected together
    with the Son
Behold the newness of life by the
    Lamb of God
Call upon His name for there is
    healing in the name of Jesus
Believe on the Son to receive your gift
    and go and tell the good news

In my Father's house are many mansions: if it were not so, I would have told you. I go to prepare a place for you.

John 14:2

If it were not so, I would have
  told you
Far greater things await you
  in my Father's house
Praise Him all the day for great
  things He has done
He is King of Kings and Lord of
  Lords, Holy is His name
You have been made victorious
  over the grave
You are joint heirs together
  with the Son
Your Father shall withhold no
  good thing from this child
Fear not, faint not for in due season
  you shall reap a harvest
God knows everything you need
  and He sees what you have done
The Most High will accomplish that
  which He has begun and reward
  you according to your works
Keep singing songs of praise, keep
  worshipping the Almighty
  for this is His delight!

The next day John seeth Jesus coming unto him,
and saith, Behold the Lamb of God, which
taketh away the sin of the world.
John 1:29

Holy, Holy, Holy,
    Holy is the Lamb
Sing praise unto Him and bless
    His holy name
He alone can heal all our
    soul's diseases
He alone is Lord and Savior of
    all who call upon Him
By His blood we have been
    redeemed
By His stripes we have been
    made whole
By His name we are called
    unto righteousness
By His Spirit we shall be
    like Him
He who has the Son shall also
    have love
This everlasting love that will
    not fail
Receive this love that you may
    impart this to those in darkness

Beloved, believe not every spirit, but try the spirits whether they are of God: because many false prophets are gone out into the world.
I John 4:1

You have this gift of discernment
    from your Father
Take heed to listen and obey as
    He speaks
Your Father would not have His
    child be ignorant
Be still, quiet and listen for the
    voice of your God
He will bring warnings of those
    seeking to do harm
He will bring great wisdom in
    times of travail
Take heed to listen and obey as
    He speaks
You will know the Spirit
    without by the Spirit within
Do not move swiftly, always
    waiting upon the Lord
You know His voice and shall
    move by His command
Be still and observe the teachings
    of Spirits from without
No harm shall come to the child
    of God for He is your keeper,
    sword, buckler and shield

Woe unto them that call evil good, and good evil;
that put darkness for light, and light for
darkness; that put bitter for sweet, and sweet
for bitter!

Isaiah 5:20

Seek the Lord's guidance
    in all things
That He may reveal unto
    you all things
You must not lean to your
    own understanding
Things are not always as
    they seem
As you draw closer to God, you
    will need more direction
There are those who would
    practice to deceive
There are those who will come to
    you in my name
They do not know me and are
    not mine
You as my child, should have no
    communion with these
Pray that they may receive the Son
    let your light shine before them
Darkness cannot comprehend
    light, Jesus is the Light
Walk in the Light to know God's
    truth and rebuke the devourer

This book of the law shall not depart out of thy mouth; but thou shalt meditate therein day and night, that thou mayest observe to do according to all that is written therein: for then thou shalt make thy way prosperous, and then thou shalt have good success.

Joshua 1:8

You shall prosper and have
much success in Jesus
He must be your Lord
over all things
You must worship and thank
Him for His sacrifice
You must honor Him with
your temple
Worship him with your whole
heart, mind and soul
Present your body a living sacrifice
and give your all to Him
You will have great success and
prosper as you yield to Him
You are not you own, but bought
with a ransom
His desire is to set you free, that
you be made whole
His desire is to heal you and restore
unto you all that was lost
Give yourself to Jesus for He is
waiting to richly bless you

But ye shall receive power, after that the Holy Ghost is come upon you: and ye shall be witnesses unto me both in Jerusalem, and in all Judaea, and in Samaria, and unto the uttermost part of the earth.

Acts 1:8

You will reign together with
the Son
Honor your Father together
with His Spirit
Seek to do all things in His
name
His name is great in heaven and
in the earth
His name is above all names and
is power
You have received this power
by His Spirit
You shall accomplish all by this
thing
Know it is the God of all creation
who has given to you this
He shall be like a medicine to the
sin sick soul
He shall be strength to those
believing on the Son
Say to the world of this awesome
power
It is God the Father who freely
giveth by the Son

**As you receive the Son, so shall you
receive His Holy Ghost power**

Promise, (14) Which is the earnest of our inheritance until the redemption of the purchased possession, unto the praise of his glory.
Ephesians 1:13-14

Holy is His name, the teacher
    of all things of your Father
Listen and heed the word of
    His Holy One
For it is by His Spirit that all
    truth shall be revealed to you
That you may know what is His
    good and perfect will
He loves you and wants to see you
    restored and made whole
Believe in the Lord and Savior, Jesus
    Christ for your healing
He has come to set you free and make
    whole your body
Rejoice in His name for whatsoever
    you ask is already done
Go and turn not again your way
    from your Father
He has created you to show forth
    His glory
Rebuke the devourer in the name of
    your Lord
Proclaim your victory by Jesus,
    the Son
Sing hallelujah, sing hallelujah, give
    God the highest praise!

But the Comforter, which is the Holy Ghost,
whom the Father will send in my name, he shall
teach you all things, and bring all things to your
remembrance, whatsoever I have said unto you.
John 14:26

Let us go, you and I in the earth
To do the will of the Father
who has sent us

For He knows His will to do
Before the foundation of the earth,
   He knew

He desires for us to be partakers with Him
He will show us what to do and by His
   power shall we do it

He will show us how to love and by His
   power shall we do it

He will show us how to give and by His
   power shall we do it

He will give to us all things and by His
   grace shall we have them

He will restore all that was lost and by His
   mercy shall we receive

Our God is Holy, Righteous and Almighty
His wonders are to behold, never ceasing

Praise ye the Lord for his mighty acts and
great works!

Now therefore hearken, O Israel, unto the statutes and unto the judgments, which I teach you, for to do them, that ye may live, and go in and possess the land which the LORD God of your fathers giveth you.
Deuteronomy 4:1

All ye soldiers of the Lord,
    gird up your loins
For the enemy draws nigh
    to thee
He shall not harm you for the
    weapons of your God are mighty

Greater is your God within you than
    the evil one
Who on that day shall be no more
    in the earth
Who on that day shall be cast into the
    lake of fire

Soldiers of the Cross, march into
    battle
Your god has given you the victory
    in Jesus
Go over and possess the land which the
    Lord, your God giveth

He shall withhold no good thing from
    His children
Every good and perfect gift cometh
    from your Father
Soldiers, march forward into the
    promises of your God

A nd whatsoever ye shall ask in my name, that will I
do, that the Father may be glorified in the Son.
John 14:13

Whatsoever things you ask in the name
of the Christ, I will do it
Prepare now the way of your Lord
that you may have room to receive
Believe on the Lord and Savior Jesus
Christ, that I raised Him from the dead
Know that He is Lord and that He being
exalted in heaven and earth is more
precious to me

Follow after Him that you may know His
ways and please your Father
You being my child and because you have
believed, you are heir together with Him
Holy and righteous is your name, but by the
Son of the Almighty God
Go now and prepare to receive gifts I will give
unto to you in the name of the Son

**_Lift up the name of Jesus for He is worthy
of all your praise!_**

Thus will I magnify myself, and sanctify myself; and I will be known in the eyes of many nations, and they shall know that I am the LORD.
Ezekiel 38:23

Wait for my Spirit to consume
you over and within
It is by Him and through Him that
you shall accomplish all
You must wait upon the Holy One
to lead you in all things of God
The Lord shall be high and lifted
up among the people
All shall behold the magnificent
glory of the Lord Jesus

You shall honor your Father by
waiting on Him
You will do things, wondrous and
mighty, that the people may
know and see He is God
To worship Him and praise Him
and bow down before Him
As the Spirit leadeth, give unto
Him your all
He will go with you to complete
the work of the Father

**Sing hallelujah, sing hallelujah
to His risen Son**

And God said unto Moses, I AM THAT I AM: and he said, Thus shalt thou say unto the children of Israel, I AM hath sent me unto you.
Exodus 3:14

I am God, the Father
    the great I Am
I am God the Son
    God in man
I am God the Holy Spirit
    God the co-laborer

I am the Most High God
    God of all the ages
I am the God who knows
    of your suffering
I am the God of power
    that you may endure

I am the God of love
    for there is none greater
I am the God of peace
    the calm in your storm
I am the God of comfort
    that hurt be driven away

I am the God of everything
    who is all and knows all
I am the God of faithfulness
    that you may be restored
I am the God of truth, that you
    may know all by my Spirit

A nd said, I cried by reason of mine affliction unto the LORD, and he heard me; out of the belly of hell cried I, and thou heardest my voice.
Jonah 2:2

L ord God, I bless your name
    for mine affliction
For through it all, I have come to
    know you in a special way
You have been there for me when
    absolutely no one else could
To soothe the doubt and to calm
    my fears

When no one else cared, I could
    cast these upon you
When I have been weak, you
    showed yourself strong
With you I feel I can do anything
    I'm in awe of your love for me
When I think of your goodness, I long
    to worship and serve you more

No greater love has a man for his friend
    than he lay down his life
You have given me your all and a love
    far beyond measure
And though I still walk with my
    affliction, your grace abounds
My Lord, I am forever indebted and
    eternally grateful to you
                    Amen

Ye have not eaten bread, neither have ye drunk wine or strong drink: that ye might know that I am the LORD your God.
Deuteronomy 29:6

You have acknowledged Me
in your ways
You have cried out to Me and
I have heard you

Your Father sees your sacrifices
of fasting and prayer
Your Father knows of your hunger
and thirst for Him
He sees you being transformed into
the likeness of the Son
He feels your heartbeat for it is
His heartbeat
He loves you and desires to give you
every good and perfect gift
Continue to covet for yourself the
best gifts and walk in His way
Thou shalt be made whole according
to thy faith

Whatsoever you ask in the name of the
resurrected Son, I shall do
Be it unto you by the power of
His blood
I stand ready to give to you these things

A nd thou shalt love the LORD thy God with all thine heart, and with all thy soul, and with all thy might.
Deuteronomy 6:5

Because Jesus Was Broken Just for Me

I declare this _____ day of _____
            Day   **Month**
in the year of our Lord, _____ that my life
                          Year
is forever changed.

It is by the Spirit of the Living God that I shall speak, move and have being. He shall be my constant companion, my joy and my strength.

I shall have no fear for great is the God of my salvation who lives in me to do His perfect will. I thank you Lord Jesus that you were wounded for me. While I can never repay you, I shall love you all my days with my whole heart, soul and might.

Unto God the Father, Son and Holy Ghost be all power, glory, honor and praise forever and ever, Amen.

_____
Signed

About the Author

The Author declares, "All that I am or would ever hope to be is but for His grace. I know that God's choosing me had nothing to do with my goodness and everything to do with His mercy. As I spend time in the presence of God, He continues to affirm that He is, why He came, and what He requires of me because He loves me so."

Having previously served as an Associate Minister of Pilgrim Rest Church of Phoenix, Arizona (Bishop Alexis A. Thomas, Senior Pastor), McDow is currently a Ministry Partner with CitiChurch International of North Scottsdale, Arizona (Dr. Terry and Judith Crist, Senior Pastors). She delights in studying and teaching biblical theology; evangelistic outreach; intercessory prayer; and providing holistic ministry solutions to individuals in need.

A licensed Gospel Minister and Board Director of the Rehoboth Community Development Corporation, a source of much joy has been serving as Director of Human Resources at the Society of St. Vincent de Paul in Phoenix, Arizona. McDow is currently enrolled at Fuller Theological Seminary while pursuing a Masters of divinity and on August 29, 2007 was named Vice President of Human Resources for HomeBase Youth Services in Phoenix, Arizona.